ANGLO~SAXONS AND VIKINGS

KS2 HISTORY KS2 HISTORY
KEY STAGE
HISTORY
KS2 HISTORY KS2 HISTORY

ANNE ROONEY

Badger Publishing Limited
Oldmeadow Road,
Hardwick Industrial Estate,
King's Lynn PE30 4JJ
Telephone: 01438 791037

www.badgerlearning.co.uk

2 4 6 8 10 9 7 5 3

Anglo-Saxons and Vikings ISBN 978-1-78464-062-0

Publisher: Susan Ross
Project editor: Paul Rockett
Design: Jo Digby Designs

Picture credits:
© Archimage / Alamy 6; © The British Library Board 16, 17, 27; © felix zaska Irish collection / Alamy 19;
© fotolincs / Alamy 20; © geogphotos / Alamy 9; © Jim Gibson / Alamy front cover, 10; © Eddie Keogh/
Reuters/Corbis 8; Mary Evans Picture Library 12, 24; The British Library/CC. Wikimedia Commons 4, 7; ©
Paul Moore / Alamy 11; King Edward the Confessor (c.1003-66) on his Deathbed, detail from the Bayeux
Tapestry, before 1082 (wool embroidery on linen), French School, (11th century) / Musee de la Tapisserie,
Bayeux, France / Bridgeman Images 22; © Richard Peel / Alamy 14; © Ted Spiegel/CORBIS 13; CC.
Wikimedia Commons 28, 29, 30.

Attempts to contact all copyright holders have been made.
If any omitted would care to contact Badger Learning, we will be happy to make
appropriate arrangements

ANGLO-SAXONS AND VIKINGS

Contents

Vocabulary

Do you know these words? Look them up in a dictionary and then see how they are used in the book.

draughty	ornate
embroidered	skirmishes
exhausted	superstitions
inherit	weary

1. Welcome to Anglo-Saxon England

Thirteen hundred years ago, England was a collection of seven small kingdoms. This was the Anglo-Saxon period.

Cornwall was part of Wales. Scotland and Ireland were separate. There were frequent small wars and skirmishes between the kingdoms.

Where was your home in Anglo-Saxon England?

2. WHO WERE THE ANGLO-SAXONS?

The Angles and Saxons came to Britain from Germany and Denmark. They arrived after Roman rule ended in Britain (410 CE).

By the 8th century, most Anglo-Saxon people were Christians, living in farming communities.

In the north, scattered farms were common. In the south, small villages formed. Houses were made of wood and thatch. They must have been damp and draughty.

Reconstruction of an Anglo-Saxon village

Religion

Monasteries were important in Anglo-Saxon England. In them, monks and nuns studied and prayed.

Printing had not yet been invented, and all books were written by hand. They were made in the monasteries, and were written in Latin, the language of the Romans.

The books were often decorated with ornate, coloured pictures and letters.

Page from the Lindisfarne Gospel, a book handwritten by Anglo-Saxon monks

Although the people were Christian, they still followed some of the practices and superstitions of earlier religions.

The dead were sometimes buried in mounds along with objects they might use in the afterlife, such as jewellery, armour and even ships.

Anglo-Saxon treasure found buried in a field in Staffordshire

HISTORY HIGHLIGHT!

One burial of a horse included the horse's armour and a bucket of food by its head!

Life for women

Women enjoyed many rights in Anglo-Saxon society. They could own property and inherit goods and money just as men could. They could rule a kingdom, and were not married against their will.

These re-enactors are mending clothes. Clothes were made by the women and girls of the family.

3. The Vikings are coming!

The Vikings were invaders and settlers from Denmark, Norway and Sweden. They were good sailors and fighters. They settled in Greenland, Italy, Spain, Russia and even North Africa.

The Vikings were fierce warriors. Their steel two-handed swords and battle-axes were terrifying and effective weapons.

They came to Britain by sea, in long boats, from the late 700s. A Viking long boat had sails and oars, and a dragon's-head prow at the front.

Vikings usually rowed through the stormy and dangerous North Sea in the summer months when the weather was better.

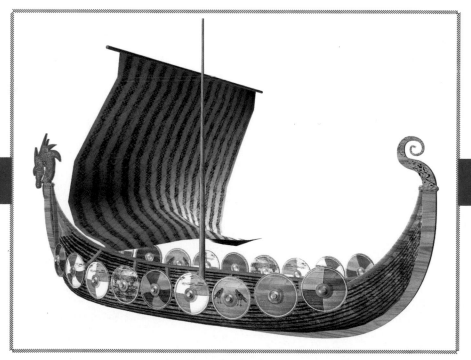

Artwork depicting a Viking long boat

Viking raids

The Vikings raided the northeast coast of England. They attacked monasteries, killing the monks and stealing treasure. They burned the wooden houses, and killed the villagers. The Anglo-Saxons grew terrified of their raids.

Vikings arriving at Lindisfarne, a small island near the northeast coast of Britain's mainland

In 793, Vikings attacked and destroyed the great monastery at Lindisfarne.

Monks left a fanciful account of it:
"Fiery dragons were seen flying in the air. A great famine immediately followed these signs, and a little after that... the ravages of heathen men miserably destroyed God's church on Lindisfarne, with plunder and slaughter."

The ruins of Lindisfarne's monastery stand behind this 9th century stone carving. It shows the Vikings coming to attack.

4. King Alfred versus the Vikings

The Viking raids continued for many years. Then in 865, instead of taking treasure and leaving, the Vikings stayed.

Within ten years, they occupied large parts of England. Only King Alfred of Wessex held out against them.

At the Battle of Edington in 878, Alfred's troops defeated the Vikings led by Guthrum. He forced Guthrum to give up the many gods of Viking religion and convert to Christianity.

Reconstruction of Anglo-Saxons and Vikings in battle

Alfred and Guthrum divided the kingdom of Mercia between them. Guthrum's part was called 'Danelaw' and covered north and east England, with a centre at York (called Jorvik).

5. Settling In

The Vikings brought their own way of life, but also adopted Anglo-Saxon ways and became integrated with the British community.

There were three levels of Viking society: thralls (nobles), karls (freemen) and jarls (serfs or slaves). Similarly, there were different levels in Anglo-Saxon society: nobles, freemen and serfs.

Life was hard and short. Half of all adult men died between 21 and 30 years of age. A third of women did not live beyond 30. There were very few medicines and people died of diseases and minor injuries.

Anglo-Saxon noblemen at a banquet, enjoying entertainment

Food and drink

People farmed wheat and barley for bread, and grew carrots, onions, cabbages, peas and beans. They cooked simple stews and porridges.

They kept pigs (for meat), sheep (for wool), cows (for milk), and chickens (for eggs). When their cows and sheep became old, they killed them, then ate the meat and used the skin.

Sheepskin was good for making warm hats, waistcoats and jackets. Leather from cows had many uses, including shoes and straps to bind round the lower legs.

Anglo-Saxon workers cutting down corn

The fields and woods provided free food: nuts, fruit, berries and wild herbs. Bees made honey, and there were fish, crabs and shellfish to eat too. People salted or dried food to keep for winter.

Viking re-enactors preparing
a family meal

HISTORY HIGHLIGHT!

People drank weak beer most of the time, because the water was often polluted.

6. And Again...

In 913, King Alfred's daughter Aethelflaed, and her brother Edward, began to win back land from the Vikings.

Anglo-Saxon rulers continued to take land from Danelaw and by 954 they controlled all of England.

But the Vikings did not give up easily. In 980, they started to raid again. The English now had a weak king, Aethelred, who agreed to pay money – called Danegeld – rather than fight the Vikings.

This coin features a picture of King Aethelred. Many of these coins have been found in Norway, as they were used as Danegeld to pay the Vikings.

In 1013, the Danish king Sweyn Forkbeard invaded. Vikings took control of England again when Cnut invaded in 1016. The Anglo-Saxons kept only Wessex.

After Cnut died, his sons ruled England. When the last of Cnut's sons died, the Anglo-Saxons came back to power and Aethelred's son Edward became king.

Edward was known as Edward the Confessor because he was very religious. Edward did not have any children. When he died, there was a struggle to take over.

Edward the Confessor on his death bed, as depicted in the Bayeux Tapestry

Timeline of Rulers from 979 to 1066

Aethelred
Anglo-Saxon king, ruled 979–1013

Sweyn Forkbeard
Viking, ruled 1013–1014

Aethelred
In power once more, ruled 1014–1016

Edmund Ironside
Son of Aethelred, ruled April–November 1016

Cnut
Son of Sweyn, ruled 1016–1035

Harold Harefoot
Son of Cnut, ruled 1035–1040

Harthacnut
Son of Cnut, ruled 1035–1042

Edward the Confessor
Son of Aethelred, ruled 1042–1066

7. A NEW ENEMY

Harold became king in 1066. He was the brother of Edward's wife. However, the Vikings and the Normans (in France) each thought they should be in charge.

Vikings from Norway attacked, landing in the north of England. Harold defeated them at Stamford Bridge in a terrible battle. Most of the Vikings were killed.

HISTORY HIGHLIGHT!

So many people died, it was said that the field was still white with bones fifty years later.

An artist's impression of the Battle of Stamford Bridge

The Battle of Hastings

But there was no time for Harold's army to rest. Just three days later, William of Normandy landed in Kent, 400 km south of where Harold and his army were.

Heavy with weapons and armour, Harold marched his exhausted army down through England towards another battle.

Already weary, the soldiers were beaten by the Normans. Harold was killed in the battle and William became king of England.

William, crowned King of England

The end of the Anglo-Saxons

William became known as William the Conqueror. He was ruthless, destroying much that was Anglo-Saxon, so that the English could not overthrow him.

William's army laid waste to great areas of land, and 100,000 people starved. They destroyed Anglo-Saxon churches and replaced them with Norman churches.

Harold's death at Hastings marked the end of the Anglo-Saxon period. William the Conqueror's attack in 1066 was the last time Britain was successfully invaded.

8. How we know

The history of Anglo-Saxon Britain was written down in the *Anglo-Saxon Chronicle*. It was started around 890, at the command of Alfred the Great, but reports events that happened as early as 60 CE.

We don't know if the information about early events is correct – the people involved had been dead a long time when it was written.

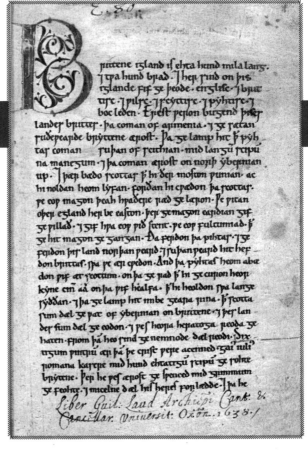

The Vikings didn't keep written records at all. All accounts of the Vikings were written by their enemies.

HISTORY HIGHLIGHT!

The Vikings used writing, called runes, only to carve inscriptions on stone.

The Battle of Hastings is recorded in an embroidered banner called the Bayeux Tapestry. It was made in England, after the Conquest.

It shows events before and after the Battle, including the death of King Harold. It is one of the most amazing accounts of a historic event ever made.

QUESTIONS

Who was responsible for making books in Anglo-Saxon England and how did they do it? *(page 7)*

What might you find in an Anglo-Saxon grave – apart from a dead Anglo-Saxon? *(page 8)*

Why did Vikings usually sail to England in the summer to carry out raids? *(page 11)*

Who did Alfred split England with after a battle in 878? *(page 15)*

Which crops did Anglo-Saxon people grow? *(page 18)*

What did the Anglo-Saxon king Aethelred pay to the Vikings to avoid fighting them? *(page 20)*

Where did King Harold defeat the Viking invaders in 1066? *(page 24)*

Which written document records the history of the Anglo-Saxon period? *(page 28)*

INDEX